ERAS TOUR OUTFITS COLORING BOOK

THIS BOOK BELONGS TO THE

ULTIMATE SWIFTIE

Published by
GRAPEVINE BOOKS

www.grapevinebooks.com
email: grapevineindiapublishers@gmail.com

Ordering Information:
Quantity sales: Special discounts are available on quantity purchases
by corporations, associations, and others.
For details, reach out to the publisher.

First published by Grapevine Books, 2025
Copyright © Grapevine, 2025

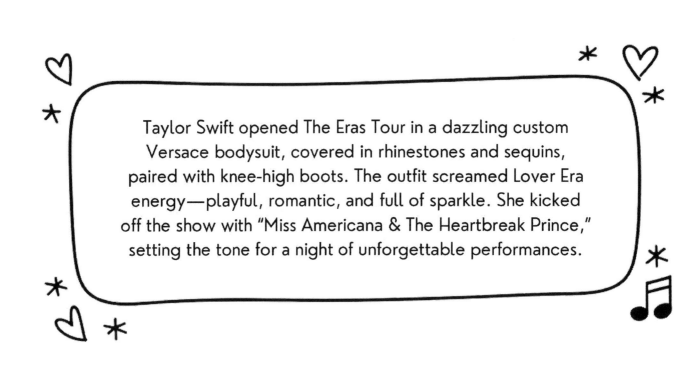

Taylor Swift opened The Eras Tour in a dazzling custom Versace bodysuit, covered in rhinestones and sequins, paired with knee-high boots. The outfit screamed Lover Era energy—playful, romantic, and full of sparkle. She kicked off the show with "Miss Americana & The Heartbreak Prince," setting the tone for a night of unforgettable performances.

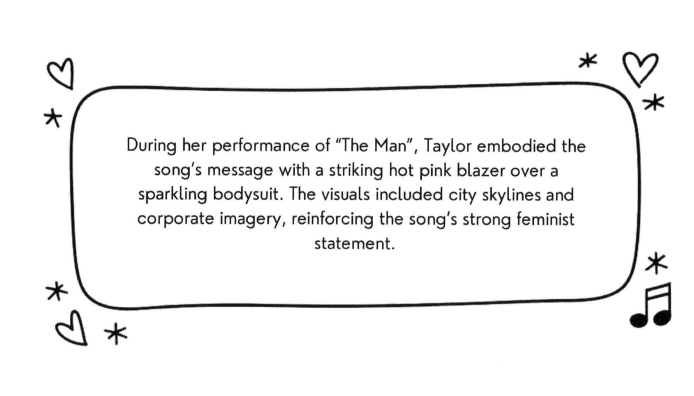

During her performance of "The Man", Taylor embodied the song's message with a striking hot pink blazer over a sparkling bodysuit. The visuals included city skylines and corporate imagery, reinforcing the song's strong feminist statement.

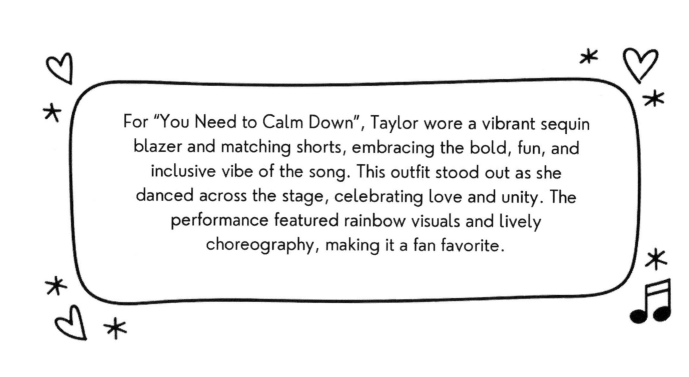

For "You Need to Calm Down", Taylor wore a vibrant sequin blazer and matching shorts, embracing the bold, fun, and inclusive vibe of the song. This outfit stood out as she danced across the stage, celebrating love and unity. The performance featured rainbow visuals and lively choreography, making it a fan favorite.

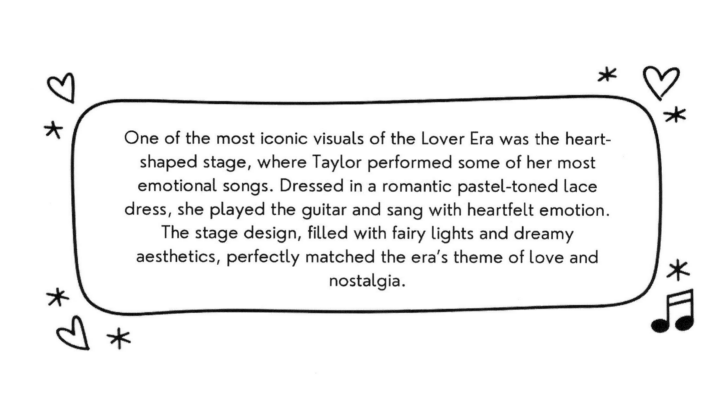

One of the most iconic visuals of the Lover Era was the heart-shaped stage, where Taylor performed some of her most emotional songs. Dressed in a romantic pastel-toned lace dress, she played the guitar and sang with heartfelt emotion. The stage design, filled with fairy lights and dreamy aesthetics, perfectly matched the era's theme of love and nostalgia.

Taylor's gold fringe dress became one of her most iconic Fearless Tour outfits! The shimmering fringe swayed as she played her guitar, making every performance feel magical. Her knee-high sparkly boots completed the look, capturing the golden glow of the Fearless era.

For her enchanting performance of "Love Story," Taylor wore a dreamy white ballgown, just like in the music video! As she sang about a forbidden love, the gown's delicate layers and elegant design made Swifties feel like they were watching a real-life fairy tale unfold.

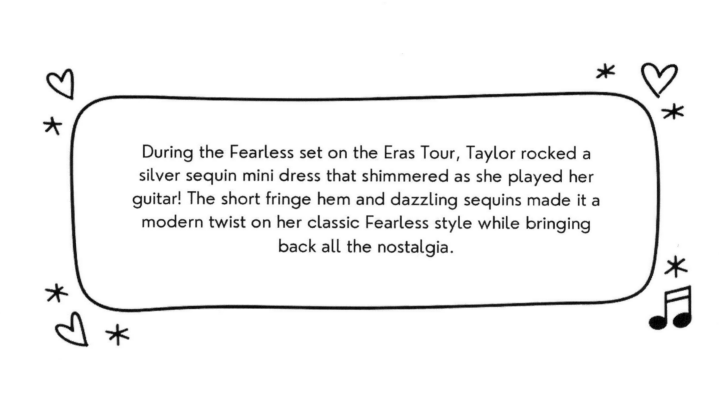

During the Fearless set on the Eras Tour, Taylor rocked a silver sequin mini dress that shimmered as she played her guitar! The short fringe hem and dazzling sequins made it a modern twist on her classic Fearless style while bringing back all the nostalgia.

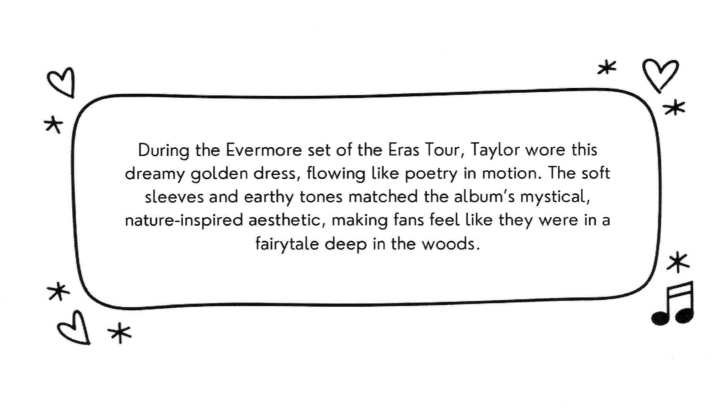

During the Evermore set of the Eras Tour, Taylor wore this dreamy golden dress, flowing like poetry in motion. The soft sleeves and earthy tones matched the album's mystical, nature-inspired aesthetic, making fans feel like they were in a fairytale deep in the woods.

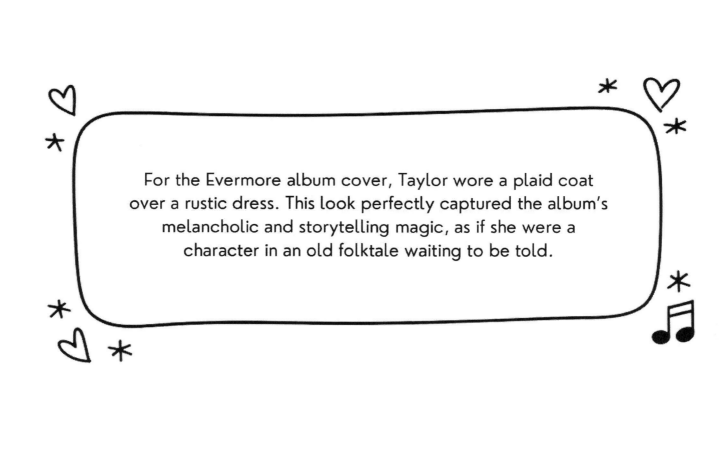

For the Evermore album cover, Taylor wore a plaid coat over a rustic dress. This look perfectly captured the album's melancholic and storytelling magic, as if she were a character in an old folktale waiting to be told.

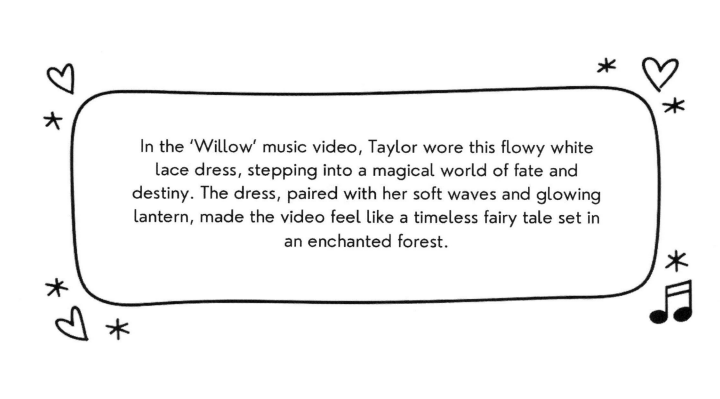

In the 'Willow' music video, Taylor wore this flowy white lace dress, stepping into a magical world of fate and destiny. The dress, paired with her soft waves and glowing lantern, made the video feel like a timeless fairy tale set in an enchanted forest.

During the Reputation set of the Eras Tour, Taylor wore this fierce black and gold bodysuit with snake patterns, symbolizing her rise from the ashes after public scrutiny. With powerful choreography and fiery visuals, this outfit perfectly captured the bold and unapologetic attitude of the Reputation era.

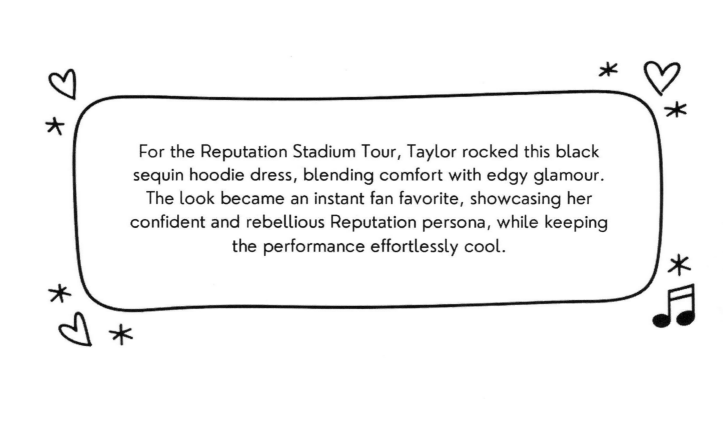

For the Reputation Stadium Tour, Taylor rocked this black sequin hoodie dress, blending comfort with edgy glamour. The look became an instant fan favorite, showcasing her confident and rebellious Reputation persona, while keeping the performance effortlessly cool.

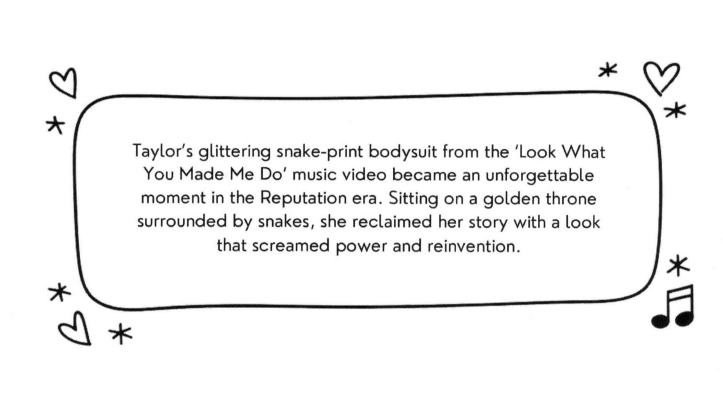

Taylor's glittering snake-print bodysuit from the 'Look What You Made Me Do' music video became an unforgettable moment in the Reputation era. Sitting on a golden throne surrounded by snakes, she reclaimed her story with a look that screamed power and reinvention.

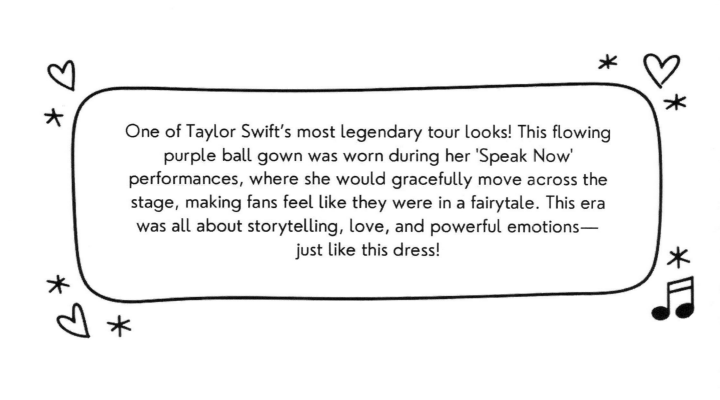

One of Taylor Swift's most legendary tour looks! This flowing purple ball gown was worn during her 'Speak Now' performances, where she would gracefully move across the stage, making fans feel like they were in a fairytale. This era was all about storytelling, love, and powerful emotions—just like this dress!

The gold fringe dress was a fan favorite, adding sparkle and movement to Taylor's high-energy performances. She wore this dress while rocking out on the guitar, proving that the Speak Now Era was full of both elegance and power!

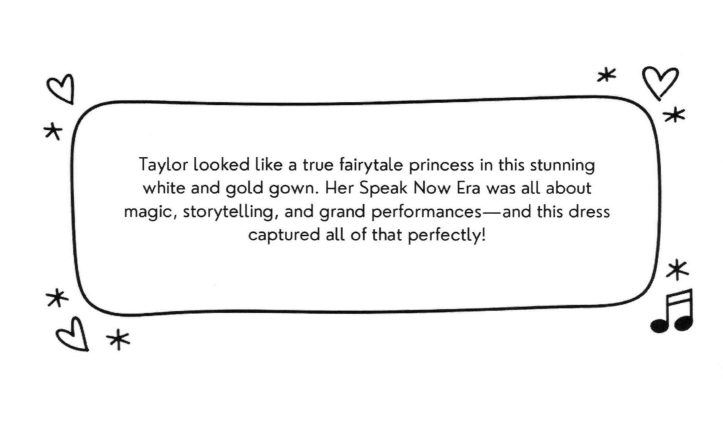

Taylor looked like a true fairytale princess in this stunning white and gold gown. Her Speak Now Era was all about magic, storytelling, and grand performances—and this dress captured all of that perfectly!

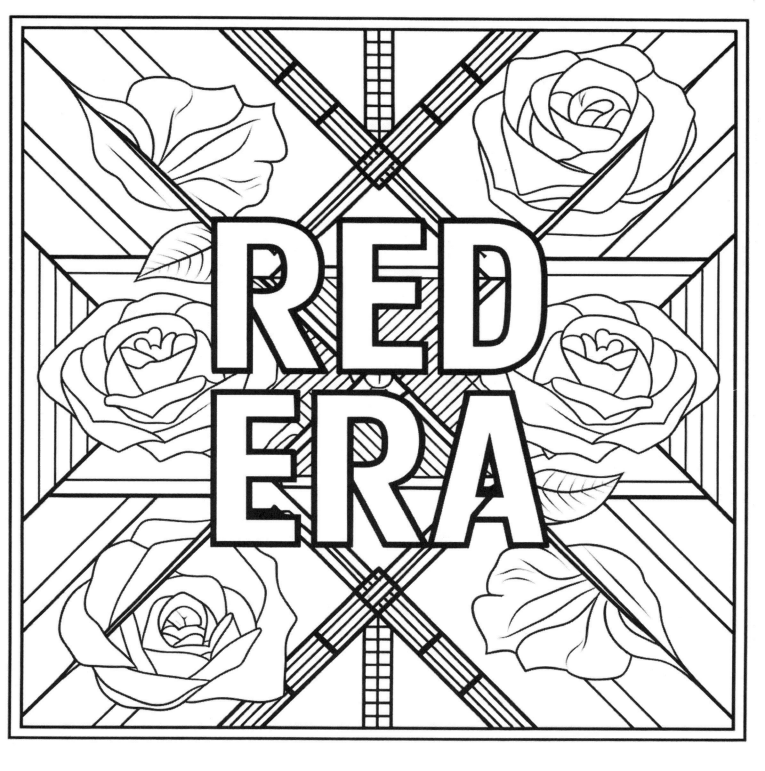

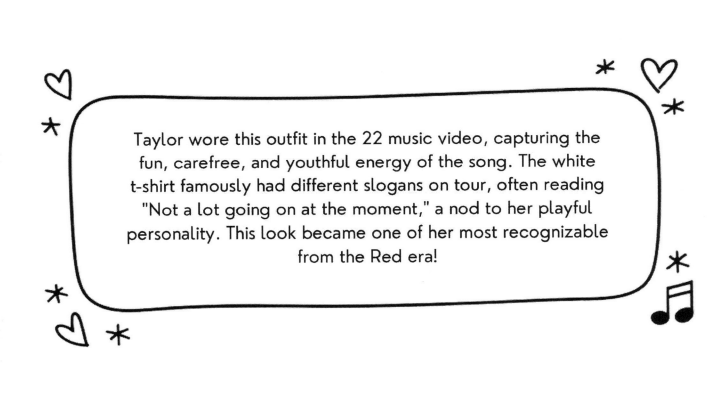

Taylor wore this outfit in the 22 music video, capturing the fun, carefree, and youthful energy of the song. The white t-shirt famously had different slogans on tour, often reading "Not a lot going on at the moment," a nod to her playful personality. This look became one of her most recognizable from the Red era!

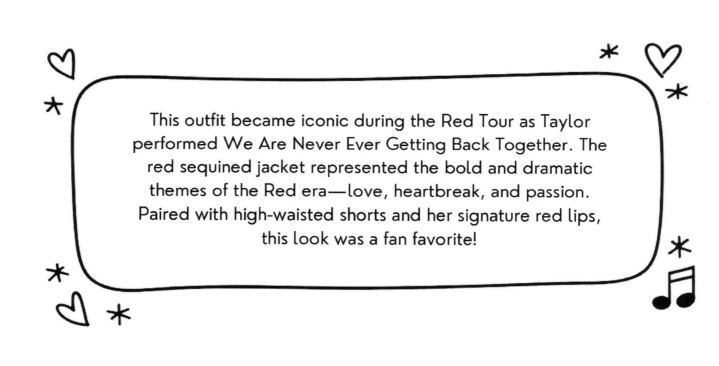

This outfit became iconic during the Red Tour as Taylor performed We Are Never Ever Getting Back Together. The red sequined jacket represented the bold and dramatic themes of the Red era—love, heartbreak, and passion. Paired with high-waisted shorts and her signature red lips, this look was a fan favorite!

During her legendary Saturday Night Live performance of All Too Well (10-Minute Version), Taylor kept it simple yet powerful. Wearing a black turtleneck and her signature red lipstick, she captivated the audience with raw emotion. This performance cemented All Too Well as one of her most iconic songs, making this outfit an unforgettable part of the Red era.

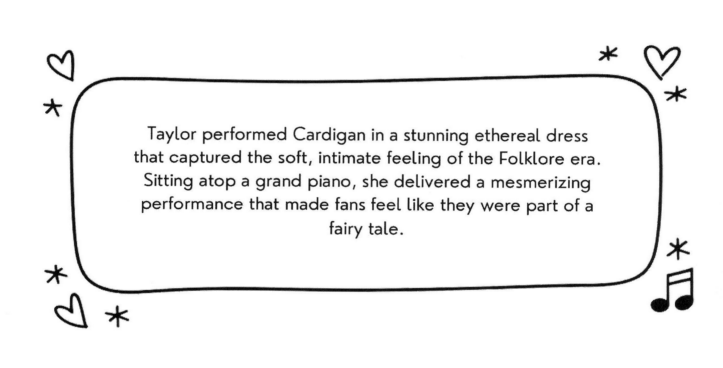

Taylor performed Cardigan in a stunning ethereal dress that captured the soft, intimate feeling of the Folklore era. Sitting atop a grand piano, she delivered a mesmerizing performance that made fans feel like they were part of a fairy tale.

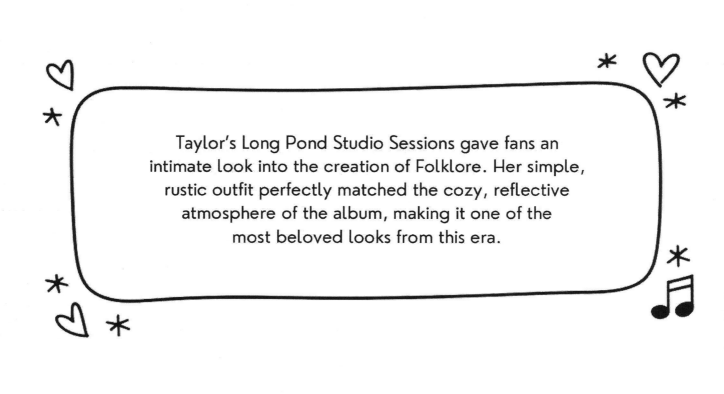

Taylor's Long Pond Studio Sessions gave fans an intimate look into the creation of Folklore. Her simple, rustic outfit perfectly matched the cozy, reflective atmosphere of the album, making it one of the most beloved looks from this era.

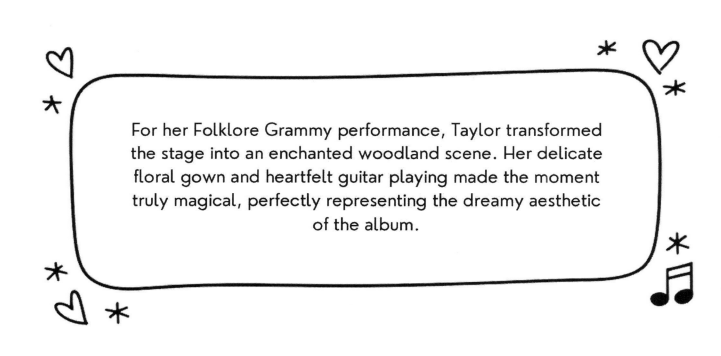

For her Folklore Grammy performance, Taylor transformed the stage into an enchanted woodland scene. Her delicate floral gown and heartfelt guitar playing made the moment truly magical, perfectly representing the dreamy aesthetic of the album.

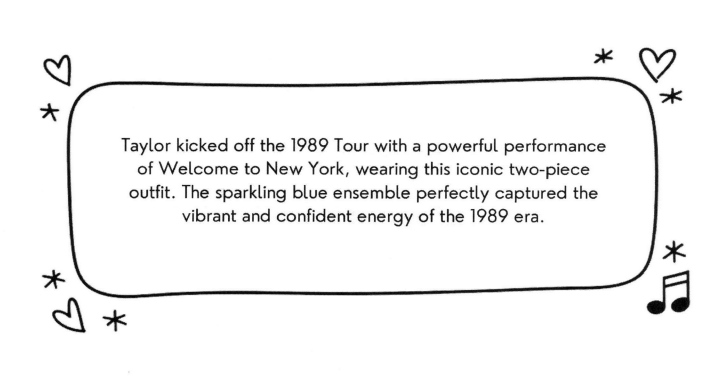

Taylor kicked off the 1989 Tour with a powerful performance of Welcome to New York, wearing this iconic two-piece outfit. The sparkling blue ensemble perfectly captured the vibrant and confident energy of the 1989 era.

Taylor's Shake It Off music video was a celebration of self-confidence and fun. Her blue-and-yellow cheerleader outfit became one of the most recognizable looks of the 1989 era, representing the song's uplifting message.

During Style, Taylor turned the stage into her personal runway. The glittering black bodysuit and her poised confidence made this one of the most iconic fashion moments of the 1989 Tour.

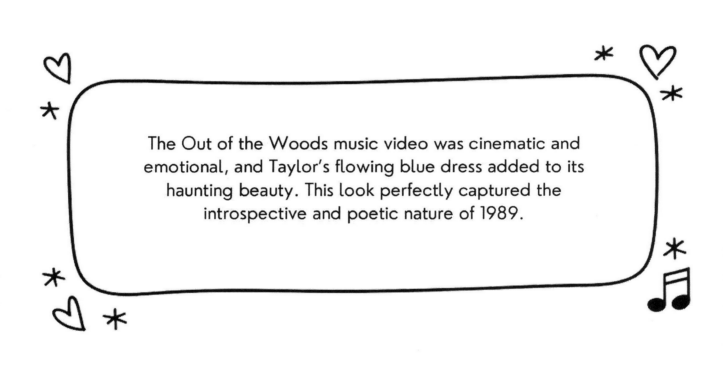

The Out of the Woods music video was cinematic and emotional, and Taylor's flowing blue dress added to its haunting beauty. This look perfectly captured the introspective and poetic nature of 1989.

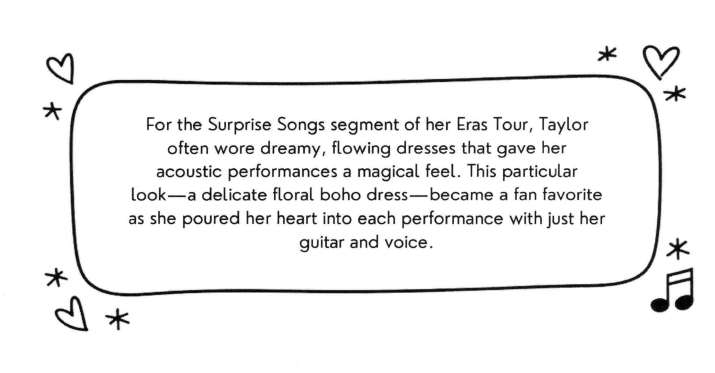

For the Surprise Songs segment of her Eras Tour, Taylor often wore dreamy, flowing dresses that gave her acoustic performances a magical feel. This particular look—a delicate floral boho dress—became a fan favorite as she poured her heart into each performance with just her guitar and voice.

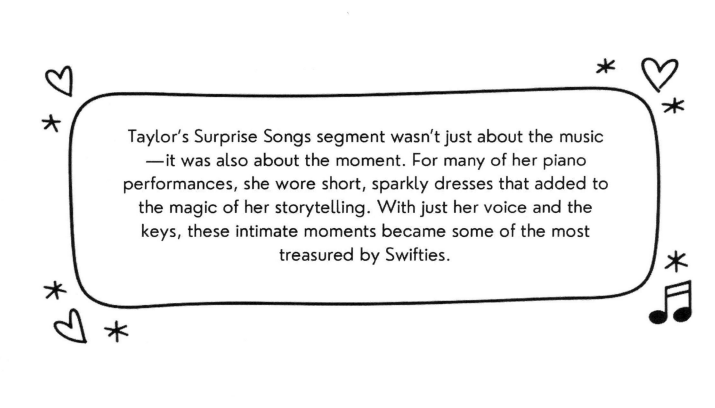

Taylor's Surprise Songs segment wasn't just about the music —it was also about the moment. For many of her piano performances, she wore short, sparkly dresses that added to the magic of her storytelling. With just her voice and the keys, these intimate moments became some of the most treasured by Swifties.

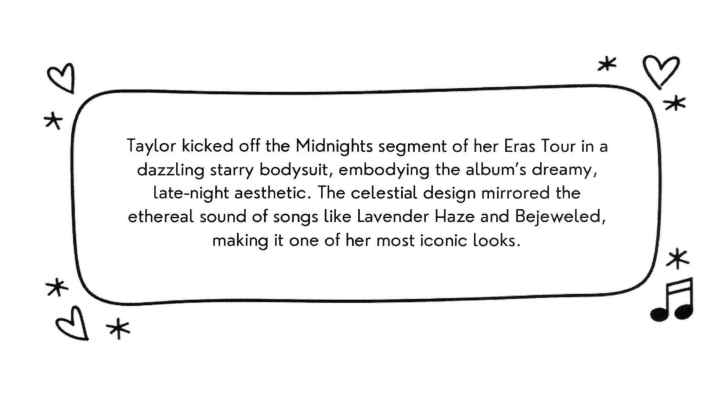

Taylor kicked off the Midnights segment of her Eras Tour in a dazzling starry bodysuit, embodying the album's dreamy, late-night aesthetic. The celestial design mirrored the ethereal sound of songs like Lavender Haze and Bejeweled, making it one of her most iconic looks.

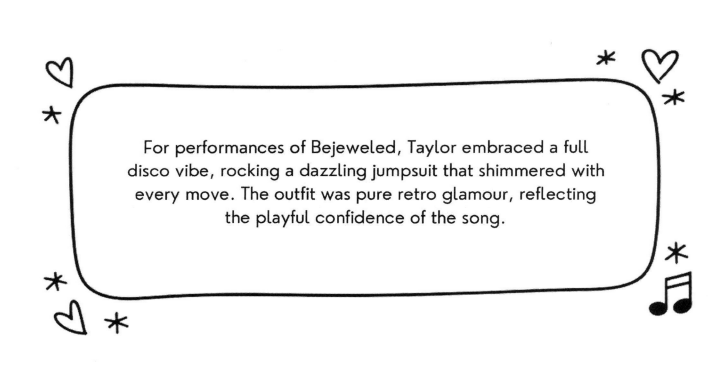

For performances of Bejeweled, Taylor embraced a full disco vibe, rocking a dazzling jumpsuit that shimmered with every move. The outfit was pure retro glamour, reflecting the playful confidence of the song.

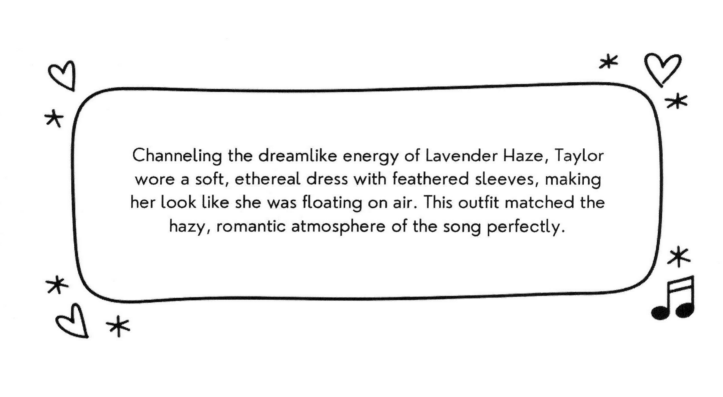

Channeling the dreamlike energy of Lavender Haze, Taylor wore a soft, ethereal dress with feathered sleeves, making her look like she was floating on air. This outfit matched the hazy, romantic atmosphere of the song perfectly.

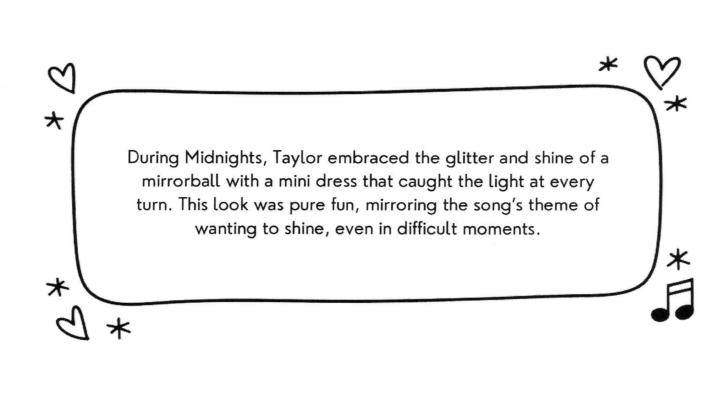

During Midnights, Taylor embraced the glitter and shine of a mirrorball with a mini dress that caught the light at every turn. This look was pure fun, mirroring the song's theme of wanting to shine, even in difficult moments.

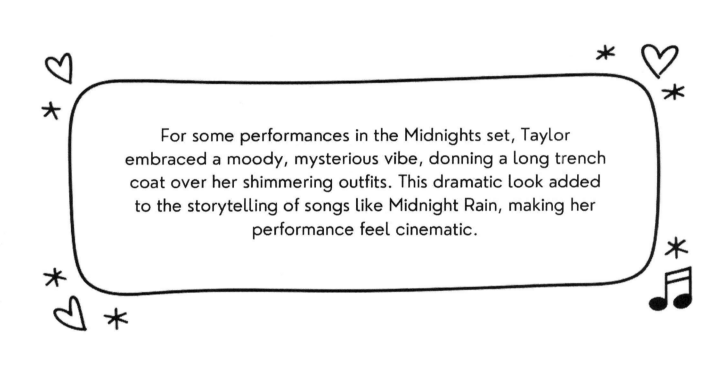

For some performances in the Midnights set, Taylor embraced a moody, mysterious vibe, donning a long trench coat over her shimmering outfits. This dramatic look added to the storytelling of songs like Midnight Rain, making her performance feel cinematic.

Made in United States
Orlando, FL
11 July 2025

62883962R00048